SCIENCE FAIR PROJECTS

Rocks and Minerals

Kelly Milner Halls

Heinemann Library
Chicago, Illinois

Designed by Kimberly R. Miracle and Fiona MacColl
Illustrations by Cavedweller Studios
Printed and bound in the United States of America, North Mankato, MN.

12 11 10
10 9 8 7 6 5 4 3 2

ISBNs: ISBN-13: 978-1-4034-7911-2(hc)   ISBN-10: 1-4034-7911-9

Library of Congress Cataloging-in-Publication Data
Halls, Kelly Milner, 1957-
  Rocks and minerals / Kelly Milner Halls.
    p. cm. -- (Science fair projects)
  Includes bibliographical references and index.
  ISBN-13: 978-1-4034-7911-2 (hc)
  1. Science projects--Juvenile literature. 2. Rocks--Juvenile literature. 3. Minerals--Juvenile
literature. I. Title.
  Q182.3.H356 2007
  552.0078--dc22

072010   005832RP   2006025461

Acknowledgments
The author and publishers are grateful to the following for permission to reproduce copyright
material: Alamy/Purestock, **p.12**; Corbis **pp. 6** (George H. H. Huey). **8** (Sygma/Sophie Elbaz),
16 (zefa/Theo Allofs), **28** (Royalty Free), **32** (Rainer Hackenberg); FLPA, **pp. 24** (Reinard
Dirschell), **30** (Nigel Cattlin), Getty Images, **pp. 11** (iconica), **18** (Photodisc), **20** (Photographers
Choice), **39** (Image Bank), **40** (Stone), **43** (National Geographic); Masterfile/Andrew Douglas,
p. 4; Science Photo Library/MAXIMILIAN STOCK LTD, **p. 36**.

Cover photograph reproduced with permission of Getty Images/Lonely Planet Images.
Background illustration by istockphoto.com.

Every effort has been made to contact copyright holders of any material reproduced
in this book. Any omissions will be rectified in subsequent printings if notice is given
to the publisher.

Disclaimer
All the Internet addresses (URLs) given in this book were valid at the time of going to press.
However, due to the dynamic nature of the Internet, some addresses may have changed, or
sites may have changed or ceased to exist since publication. While the author and publisher
regret any inconvenience this may cause readers, no responsibility for any such changes can
be accepted by either the author or the publisher.

» Some words are shown in bold, **like this**. You can
find the definitions for these words in the glossary.

Contents

Science Fair Basics   **4**

PROJECTS:

Hard Rock   **8**

Acid and Erosion   **12**

So Smooth   **16**

Soak It Up   **20**

It's Raining, It's ... Soaking?   **24**

Drink Your Minerals   **28**

Rock and Boil   **32**

Canned Minerals   **36**

A Dirty Business   **40**

The Competition   **44**

Glossary   **47**

Index   **48**

Science Fair Basics

Starting a science fair project can be an exciting challenge. You can test **scientific theory** by developing an appropriate scientific question. Then you can search, using the thoughtful steps of a well-planned experiment, for the answer to that question. It's like a treasure hunt of the mind.

In a way, your mission is to better understand how your world and the things in it work. You may be rewarded with a good grade or an award for your scientific hard work. But no matter what scores your project receives, you'll be a winner. That's because you will know a little bit more about your subject than you did before you started.

In this book, we'll look at nine different science fair projects related to rocks and minerals. We will explore the amazing rocks and minerals that make up our Earth and learn more about their properties and Earth's **geologic** history.

Do Your Research

Is there something about rocks and minerals you've always wondered about? Something you don't quite understand but would like to? Then do a little research about the subject. Go to the library and check out books about the subject that interests you.

Use your favorite Internet search engine to find reliable online sources. Museums, universities, scientific journals, newspapers, and magazines are among the best sources for accurate research. Each experiment in this book lists some suggestions for further research.

When doing research you need to make sure your sources are reliable. Ask yourself the following questions about sources, especially those you find online.

The Experiments

The beginning of each experiment contains a box like this.

Possible Question:

This question is a suggested starting point for your experiment. You will need to adapt the question to reflect your own interests.

Possible Hypothesis:

Don't worry if your hypothesis doesn't match the one listed here, this is only a suggestion.

Approximate Cost of Materials:

Discuss this with your parents before beginning work.

Materials Needed:

Make sure you can easily get all of the materials listed and gather them before beginning work.

Level of Difficulty:

There are three levels of experiments in this book: Easy, Intermediate, and Hard. The level of difficulty is based on how long the experiment takes and how complicated it is.

1) How old is the source? Is it possible that the information is outdated?

2) Who wrote the source? Is there an identifiable author, and is the author qualified to write about the topic?

3) What is the purpose of the source? The website of a potato chip company is probably not the best place to look for information on healthful diets.

4) Is the information well documented? Can you tell where the author got his or her information?

Some websites allow you to "chat" online with experts. Make sure you discuss this with your parent or teacher before participating. Never give out private information, including your address online.

Once you know a little more about the subject you want to explore, you'll be ready to ask a science project question and form an intelligent **hypothesis**. A hypothesis is an educated guess about what the results of your experiment will be. Finally, you'll be ready to begin your science fair exploration!

Continued

What Is an Experiment?

When you say you're going to "experiment" you may just mean that you're going to try something out. When a scientist uses that word though, he or she means something else. In a proper experiment, you have **variables** and a **control**. A variable is something that changes. The independent variable is the thing you purposely change as part of the experiment. The dependent variable is the change that happens in response to the thing you do. The controlled variables, or control group, are the things you do not change so that you have something to compare your outcomes to. Here's an example: Ten people have headaches. You give 5 people (Group A) asprins. You do not allow 5 people (Group B) to do anything for their headaches. Group A is the independent variable. The effects of the asprins are the dependent variable. Group B is a control group. To make sure the experiment is accurate though, you need to do it several times.

Some of the projects in this book are not proper experiments. They are projects designed to help you learn about a subject. You need to check with your teacher about whether these projects are appropriate for your science fair. Make sure you know all the science fair rules about what kinds of projects and materials are allowed before beginning.

How did these rocks form? What causes their striking colors?

Your Hypothesis

Once you've decided what question you're going to try to answer, you'll want to make a scientific **prediction** of what you'll discover through your science project. For example, if you wonder why rocks have different colors, your question might be "Can one rock be made of more than one mineral?"

Remember, a hypothesis is an educated guess about how your experiment will turn out—what results you'll observe. So your hypothesis in response to the above question might be, "Each rock is made of different minerals." The hypothesis is your best guess of how things might turn out when the experiment has been completed. It's also a good way to find out if you can actually complete the steps needed to answer your project question. If your question is, "How many rocks are on Mount Rushmore?," it will be impossible to prove your hypothesis, no matter what you make it. So, be sure the evidence to prove or disprove your hypothesis is actually within reach.

Research Journal

It is very important to keep careful notes about your project. From start to finish, make entries in your research journal so you won't have to rely on memory when it comes time to create your display. What time did you start your experiment? How long did you work on it each day? What were the variables, or things that changed, about your experimental setting? How did they change and why? What things did you overlook in planning your project? How did you solve the problems, once you discovered them?

These are the kinds of questions you'll answer in your research journal. No detail is too small when it comes to scientific research. You'll find some tips on writing your report and preparing a great display at the back of this book on pages 44–46. Use these and the tips in each project as guides, but don't be afraid to get creative. Make your display, and your project, your own.

Hard Rock

Rocks are hard right? But are all rocks equally hard? Mohs scale of hardness is one way scientists classify minerals. Rocks are made up of minerals. Can the Mohs scale be applied to rocks? This project will help you find out.

Do Your Research

This project deals with rock classification. This is not an experiment, but a research project. Talk to your teacher about whether or not this is appropriate for your science fair. After you do some research on minerals, rocks, and classification systems, you will be ready to tackle this project, or one of your own.

Here are some books and websites you could start with in your research:

» *DK/Google E.guides: Rocks and Minerals.* New York: DK, 2005.
» Pellant, Chris. *Smithsonian Handbooks: Rocks and Minerals.* New York: DK, 2005.
» American Federation of Mineralogical Societies: http://www.amfed.org/t_mohs.htm
» Mineralogical Society of America: http://www.minsocam.org/

Project Information

Possible Question:

Are all rocks equally hard?

Possible Hypothesis:

Different kinds of rocks will have different levels of hardness.

Level of Difficulty:

Intermediate

Approximate Cost of Materials:

$5

Materials Needed:

» Eight different kinds of rock found around your house or school. If you cannot find rocks that look different from each other, consider buying some rocks from a gardening or craft store.

» Household nail

» Table knife (use with adult supervision)

» A piece of glass, such as a mirror (make sure to get permission as the project may damage the mirror)

» A camera and film, or digital camera (optional)

» Glue (optional)

» Small pieces of posterboard (optional)

Steps to Success:

1. Study the Mohs hardness scale.

2. Collect or buy eight different rocks. The rocks do not have to be anything special, so do not spend a lot of money.

3. Arrange the rocks in what you believe to be their correct order, with the softest rock first and the hardest rock last. Draw (or place a photograph) of each rock in your research journal. Under the picture of the rock, make a guess of where you think it is on the Mohs scale. Leave room to write in the results of your experiment.

Continued

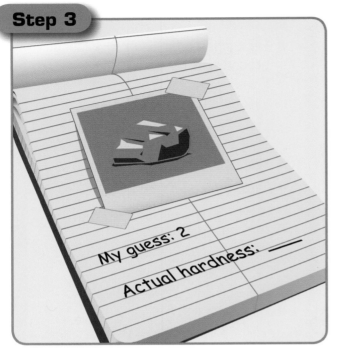

My guess: 2

Actual hardness: _____

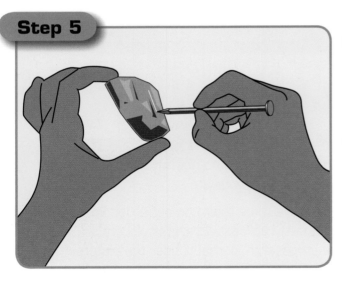

4. Attempt to scratch the rock with your fingernail. If your fingernail leaves a mark, the rock is a 2.

5. If your fingernail does not leave a mark, move on to scratching the rock with a household nail, then a knife. Make sure you scrape away from yourself so that you do not get dust in your eye. Scraping away from your body will also protect you if the knife or nail slips. Use the Mohs scale to determine the hardness of the rock based on what leaves a scratch on it. Once you have left a mark on the rock, you do not need to mark it with other substances.

ADULT SUPERVISION REQUIRED

6. If the knife does not leave a mark, attempt to use the rock to mark on the piece of glass.

ADULT SUPERVISION REQUIRED

7. Repeat steps 4–6 with each rock that you collect.

Added Activities to Give Your Project Extra Punch:

» Attempt to scratch the softer rocks with the harder rocks and the harder rocks with the softer rocks. What happens?
» If a rock has different colors it means it is made up of different minerals. Apply the test to different areas of the rock and see if you get different results. How does this affect your classification system?
» Develop a different classification system for the rocks. For example, can they be classified by their color?
» Use a field guide to determine what kind of rock you were testing.

Display Extras:

» Glue the rocks onto small pieces of posterboard and write down your hypothesis, and your end result. Include these in your display.
» Pictures of rocks of various hardness levels.
» Charts showing different classification systems.

Diamonds are a mineral. The diamond is a 10 on the Mohs scale. Why is this important to know?

Acid and Erosion

Acid rain is the term used to describe any precipitation that has acidic **pollutants** in it. What effect do these acids have on rocks and erosion? Is acid rain changing the world around us?

Do Your Research

This project deals with chemicals and erosion. Before you begin your project do some research to find out more about acid rain, erosion, and the different ways erosion occurs. Once you've done some research you can tackle this project, or you may come up with your own unique project after you've read and learned more about the topic.

Here are some books and websites you could start with in your research:

» Capstone Press Editors. *Acid Rain*. Mankato, MN: Capstone Press, 2002.

» Gifford, Clive. *Pollution*. Chicago: Heinemann Library, 2005.

» EPA: Acid Rain Student Site:
http://www.epa.gov/acidrain/site_students/index.html

Project Information

Possible Question:

Does acid cause erosion?

Possible Hypothesis:

Acid can cause erosion.

Level of Difficulty:	Approximate Cost of Materials:
Easy	$15

Materials Needed:

» 10 limestone chips
» 2 jars with lids
» 2 bowls
» Water
» Vinegar
» Kitchen scale

Steps to Success:

1. Divide limestone chips into two piles of five each. Weigh each pile and record the results. Place one pile in each container.

2. Pour water over the chips in one jar. Cover the jar and label it "water."

3. Pour the same amount of vinegar over the other chips. Cover the jar and label it "vinegar."

Step 3

Continued

4. Leave the jars overnight.

5. The next day pour the liquid out of the "water" jar into a bowl.
Label that bowl "water."

6. Pour the liquid out of the "vinegar" jar into a bowl.
Label that bowl "vinegar."

7. Compare the liquid in the bowls.

8. Weigh the chips and record the results.

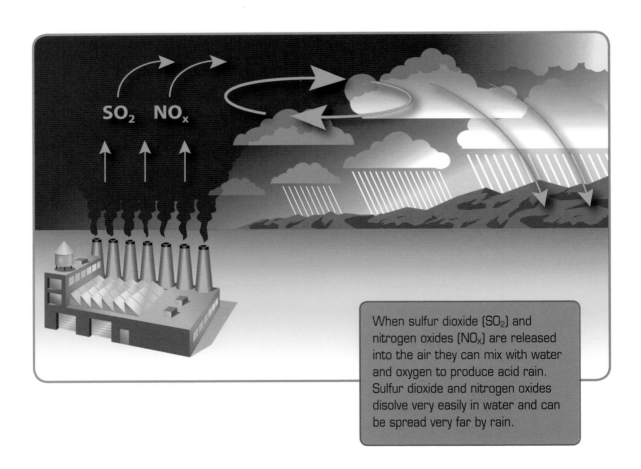

SO_2 NO_x

When sulfur dioxide (SO_2) and nitrogen oxides (NO_x) are released into the air they can mix with water and oxygen to produce acid rain. Sulfur dioxide and nitrogen oxides disolve very easily in water and can be spread very far by rain.

Result Summary:

» Does one bowl have more solid material in it than the other?

» Do the limestone chips look different?

» Did the weight of either set of chips change?

Added Activities:

» Repeat the experiment with different kinds of rock.

» Based on your research, explain why the quicker erosion in vinegar is a problem.

Display Extras:

» Save the liquid in a covered container and display it.

» Display the limestone chips.

So Smooth

Some rocks are sharp enough to be used as knife-like weapons. Some are smooth enough to use as tabletops. Are these the same rocks? Can a sharp rock become smooth naturally? How long would that take? This experiment may help you find out how to smooth out those rough rocky edges.

Do Your Research

This project deals with rocks and weather. This project requires a certain amount of physical strength and takes 30 days to complete. Make sure you have enough time to complete it. Before you begin your project do some research to find out more about different kinds of rocks and how weather and other forces affect rocks. Once you've done some research you can tackle this project, or you may come up with your own unique project after you've read and learned more about the topic.

Here are some books and websites you could start with in your research:

» *DK/Google E.guides: Rocks and Minerals.* New York: DK, 2005.
» Pellant, Chris. *Smithsonian Handbooks: Rocks and Minerals.* New York: DK, 2005.
» RocksForKids.com: http://www.rocksforkids.com/RFK/TableofContents.html
» KidsConnect.com Rocks & Minerals: http://www.kidskonnect.com/RocksMinerals/RocksMineralsHome.html

Project Information

Possible Question:

How do sharp rocks get smooth?

Possible Hypothesis:

Natural elements like wind and water smooth sharp rocks.

Level of Difficulty:

Easy

Approximate Cost of Materials:

$10

Materials Needed:

» Five sharp rocks about three inches long. The rocks should be as similar as possible.
» Three small containers with lids
» Permanent marker
» Sandpaper
» Gardening gloves
» Egg timer or alarm clock
» Camera and film or digital camera
» Newspaper

Steps to Success:

1. Mark each rock with a 1, 2, 3, 4, or 5.

2. Photograph your rocks before you begin the experiment.

3. In your research journal, take careful notes about how sharp each rock is, and what it looks like.

4. Over a piece of newspaper, sand the sharp end of rock number 1 for five minutes. Make sure not to sand over the number you have written on the rock. Set your timer or alarm clock to make sure you sand for exactly five minutes.

5. Collect any dust in a container marked with a 1.

Step 5

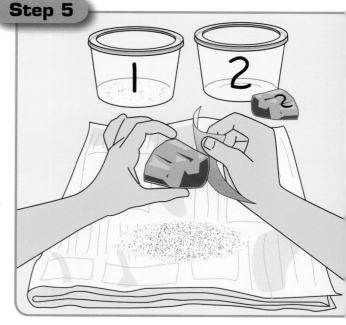

Continued

6. Rinse the rock in cool tap water for exactly 60 seconds.

7. Repeat steps 4 and 5 with rock number 2. However, do NOT rinse this rock.

8. With rock number 3, rinse it, but do not use sandpaper on it.

9. Put rock number 4 in a small container labeled 4. Fill the container with water, put the lid on it and move it to a safe place. Do not touch it for the rest of the experiment. Put rock number 5 in a safe place as well, and do not touch it.

10. Repeat the entire experiment on rocks 1, 2, and 3 every day for 30 days. Make careful notes about any changes you notice in any of the rocks.

11. Photograph the rocks at the end of the 30 days.

12. Compare all 5 rocks.

Humans formed these rocks into weapons. Could they have gotten this sharp on their own?

Added Activities to Give Your Project Extra Punch:

» Weigh the stones before and after each sanding period. Compare the change in the weight of the stone to the weight of the dust collected.

» Repeat the experiment on different kinds of rocks.

» Repeat the experiment using different temperatures of water.

Display Extras:

» Display your 5 rocks and sandpaper.

» Display the dust containers.

» Display all the photographs you took, along with photographs from magazines illustrating erosion in nature, both by water and wind.

» Provide sandpaper, water, and a rock for people to recreate the experiment.

Soak It Up

What things in everyday life are **absorbent**? What things soak up water or other liquids? Sponges? Paper towels? Rocks? It's true. They may seem like the ultimate solids, but even rocks have microscopic **pores**. And this experiment will prove it.

Do Your Research

This project deals with **sedimentary** rocks and porosity. Before you begin your project, do some research on the different kinds of rocks and their characteristics. Once you've done some research you can tackle this project. Or, you may come up with your own unique project.

Here are some books and websites you could start with in your research:

» *DK/Google E.guides: Rocks and Minerals*. New York: DK, 2005.

» Pellant, Chris. *Smithsonian Handbooks: Rocks and Minerals*. New York: DK, 2005.

» Rock Hounds: How Sedimentary Rocks Are Formed: http://www.fi.edu/fellows/fellow1/oct98/create/sediment.htm

» Physical Geography.net: Characteristics of Sedimentary Rocks: http://www.physicalgeography.net/fundamentals/10f.html

» United States Geological Survey: Sedimentary Rocks: http://wrgis.wr.usgs.gov/docs/parks/rxmin/rock2.html

Project Information

Possible Question:

Can rocks hold water?

Possible Hypothesis:

Yes, rocks can hold water.

Level of Difficulty:	Approximate Cost of Materials:
Hard	$20

Materials Needed:

» 1 medium size rock (A sedimentary rock such as sandstone or pumice will work better for this experiment. If you use pumice you will need to anchor it in the water, because it floats.)

» 2 jars large enough to fit the rock into

» 3 cups of water

» 3 cups of uncooked rice or beans

» A ruler

» Masking tape

» A string and bolt (if you use pumice)

Steps to Success:

1. Fill one jar with water. Visually check to see if there will be enough water to cover the rock. If not, add more water.

2. Fill the second jar with rice up to the same level as the water in the first jar.

3. Use a piece of masking tape on each jar to mark the top level of the rice and water.

Step 3

Continued ▷

4. Carefully place the rock in the rice. If you are using pumice, attach the bolt as described in step 8 below before placing it in the jar. This way you will be putting the same volume in each jar.

5. Use the masking tape to mark exactly where the rice now comes to.

6. Measure the distance between the two pieces of tape. Make sure to measure exactly and make a note of your measurement.

7. Gently place your rock into the water so it is completely submerged.

Step 8

8. If you are testing pumice, a volcanic rock that floats, tie a thread or string around the sample and anchor it with a metal nut or bolt, so it will stay under the water. Wait 5 minutes.

9. Use the masking tape to mark exactly where the water now comes to.

10. Measure the distance between the two pieces of tape.

11. Compare the difference between the amount the rice rose and the amount the water rose. If the water did not rise as high as the rice, that means the rock absorbed some of the water.

Result Summary:

» Did your rock absorb any water?

» Would other rocks have absorbed more or less water? Why?

» What else might rocks absorb? Consider oil, for example; is that absorbed into rocks?

Added Activities to Give Your Project Extra Punch:

» Repeat the same experiment with inexpensive cooking oil.

» Repeat the experiment with salt water, and see if it changes the measurements.

» Consider other ways of measuring the absorption. Would weighing the rocks work?

Display Extras:

» Display pictures of different kinds of rock with their names and classifications.

It's Raining, It's ... Soaking?

Can you walk on water? You might not think so but you probably do every day. Underneath the land you see are rocks, and some of the space between those rocks is filled by water. The water is rainwater that has soaked through the ground. The geologic formation that holds the water is known as an **aquifer**. What makes the best aquifer? In this project you will attempt to create your own aquifer recipe.

Do Your Research

This project is about aquifers. Before you begin your project do some research to find out more about rainwater, water tables, and aquifers. Once you have done some research, you can tackle this project. Or, you may come up with your own unique project after you've read and learned more about the subject.

Here are some books and websites you could start with in your research:

» Harman, Rebecca. *The Water Cycle*. Chicago: Heinemann Library, 2005.

» Parker, Steve. *The Science of Water: Projects and Experiments with Water Science and Power*. Chicago: Heinemann Library, 2005.

» U.S. Geological Society: Water Science for Schools: http://ga.water.usgs.gov/edu

Project Information

Possible Question:

What materials hold water well?

Possible Hypothesis:

A combination of materials will do the best job of holding water.

Level of Difficulty:

Intermediate

Approximate Cost of Materials:

$5

Materials Needed:

» Several large, disposable cups (preferably clear; all cups should be the same size)
» Bowls or containers wider than the cups
» 2–4 craft sticks
» Measuring spoons and cups
» Water
» Clay
» Dirt
» Rocks
» Sand
» Other natural materials, such as sticks and leaves (optional)
» Other human-made materials, such as paper and plastic wrap (optional)

Steps to Success:

1. **NOTE:** This project can get messy. Make sure to cover your clothes and workspace.

2. Research aquifers to try and determine what combination of your materials will do the best job of holding water.

3. Punch a small hole in the bottom of a cup. Label the cup "1."

4. Fill the cup about halfway up with a combination of clay, dirt, rocks, and sand. Use your measuring cups and spoons so that you know exactly how much of each material is in the cup. Keep careful and precise notes.

Continued

fill line

1

5. Mark a line on the cup to show how high you filled it.

6. Place the cup on the craft sticks over the container.

7. Slowly and carefully pour 1/2 cup of water into the cup.

8. Observe what happens to the water. Does it run out immediately? Does it pool at the top of the cup? Make careful notes of the time it takes for the water to run out or pool at the top.

9. If the water does not run out or pool at the top, slowly add another 1/2 cup of water and see what happens.

10. Use your measuring cups and spoons to carefully determine how much water ran out or pooled at the top.

11. Repeat the experiment as many times as desired in different cups. Make sure to fill each cup to the exact same point. Change the proportions of the ingredients each time. Your goal is to find a combination that holds water.

A chart like this will help you determine which recipe is best.

Ingredients	Mixtures				
	1	2	3	4	5
	1/4 cup sand 1/4 cup rocks	1/8 cup sand 1/4 cup rocks			
Results					

Result Summary:

» Did you create a successful recipe?

» What recipe worked the best?

» How much water was lost in the unsuccessful recipes?

» Were the changes required small or large?

Added Activities to Give Your Project Extra Punch:

» Repeat the experiment with leaves, sticks, or other natural materials.

» Repeat the experiment with human-made materials mixed in with the natural materials.

Display Extras:

» An explanation of aquifers and why they are important.

» An explanation of the importance of groundwater.

» Photos of naturally occurring aquifers.

» Your cups with the ingredients still in them.

Drink Your Minerals

Plants depend on minerals in the water to grow and to be healthy. Table salt is a mineral called halite that is often naturally found in soil, especially near oceans. So what happens when you add extra salt to a plant's water? Will it thrive or get sick?

Do Your Research

This project deals with salt and other minerals. Before you begin your project, do some research to find out more about salt, as well as other minerals. Once you've done some research, you can tackle this project. Or, you may come up with your own unique project after you've read and learned more about the topic.

Here are some books and websites you could start with in your research:

» Cobb, Allan B. *Super Science Projects About Oceans*. New York: Rosen, 2005.

» Water Science for Schools: http://www.ga.water.usgs.gov/edu/

» The EPA's Office of Water: htttp://www.epa.gov/ow/kids,html

» Mineralogical Society of America: http://www.minsocam.org/MSA/collectors_corner/faq/faqmingen.htm

Project Information

Possible Question:

Does adding minerals to water always help plants?

Possible Hypothesis:

Too much of a mineral can harm a plant.

Level of Difficulty:

Easy

Approximate Cost of Materials:

$20

Materials Needed:

» 2 identical six-inch plants, it is best to buy new plants from the same store to make sure they are identical.

» Two 2-liter plastic bottles with lids

» 2 liters of distilled water

» Table salt

» Sunny place by the window for both plants

» Camera and film or digital camera (optional)

Steps to Success:

1. Place both plants side-by-side in a warm, sunny window.

2. Mark one of the plant's plastic pots with the word "salt" and the other with the word "plain."

3. In your research journal make notes about the plants' appearance. Make sure to write down any imperfections or problems you see with the plants. Take a picture of both plants.

 Continued

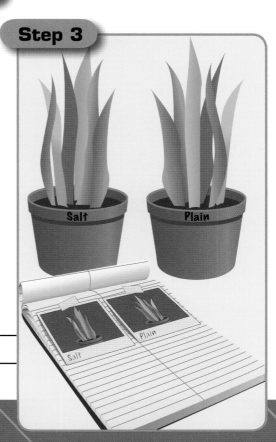

Step 3

4. Mix 1 liter of distilled water and 1 cup table salt in the first plastic bottle.

5. Fill the second plastic bottle with 1 liter of plain distilled water.

6. Water each plant with 1/8 a cup of liquid every other day—the salty solution for the "salt" plant, the plain water for the "plain" plant.

7. Do not move the plants. Keep them in the same place for the entire duration of the experiment.

8. Each time you water the plant, take notes on any changes you observe, even if your note says, "no change."

9. At the end of two weeks, take detailed notes about any differences you observe in the plants.

Was this house plant murdered by salt?

Result Summary:

» Was the plant watered with salt solution damaged in any way?

» Did the plants both grow equally?

» Has the color of the plants changed?

» Has the shape or thickness of the leaves changed?

» What does the surface of the soil look like in both pots?

Added Activities to Give Your Project Extra Punch:

» Dissolve a mineral supplement like iron or zinc in water and repeat the experiment using that water instead of salt water. Make sure to keep any supplements away from small children.

» Repeat the experiment using commercial plant food mixed as directed and plain water and record the differences. Make a note of the minerals in the plant food.

Display Extras:

» Your plants, even if one or both are no longer in good health.

» Books on plant care.

» Design your display to look like a garden or garden store

Rock and Boil

A bottle of "mineral water" can be an expensive drink. What effect do minerals actually have on water? For example, can they change the speed at which water boils? This project will show you.

Do Your Research

This project deals with minerals and their effects. Before you begin your project, do some research to find out more about minerals. Once you've done some research, you can tackle this project. Or, you may come up with your own unique project after you've read and learned more about the topic.

Here are some books and websites you could start with in your research:

» *DK/Google E.guides: Rocks and Minerals*. New York: DK, 2005.
» Pellant, Chris. *Smithsonian Handbooks: Rocks and Minerals*. New York: DK, 2005.
» How to Identify Minerals (San Diego Natural History Museum): http://www.sdnhm.org/kids/minerals/how-to.html
» Identification of Rocks and Minerals: http://www.rocksforkids.com/RFK/identification.html
» Boiling Point of Water Calculator: http://www.biggreenegg.com/boilingPoint.htm

Project Information

Possible Question:

Will water come to a boil faster with rocks in the pan?

Possible Hypothesis:

Water will come to a boil faster with rocks in the pan.

Level of Difficulty:

Easy

Approximate Cost of Materials:

$10

Materials Needed:

» One 2-quart sauce pan
» 5 clean 2-inch rocks of the same type (use a rock identification guide to help you)
» 2 quarts of mineral-free distilled water
» Stovetop burner
» Adult supervision
» Stopwatch

Steps to Success:

1. Put 1 quart of water in your pan.

2. Add your five rocks to the water in the pan.

3. Put your pan, rocks, and water on a burner on the stove.

ADULT SUPERVISION REQUIRED

4. Turn the burner to high.

5. Start your stopwatch.

Step 2

Continued

33

6. When the water boils, stop the timer and record the minutes and seconds it took for the water to boil with the rocks. You will know your water is boiling when you see a lot of bubbles in the middle of the pan.

7. Allow the pan and contents to cool.

8. Replace the previously used water with fresh water.

9. Repeat steps 1 through 7, except this time omit the rocks from your saucepan and water.

10. If possible, use a field guide to research the mineral composition of your rocks. This may not be possible with rocks found on the street.

Result Summary:

» Did the water with the rocks boil more quickly than the water without the rocks?

» Did the water change color, and if so was it due to the minerals? What minerals may have caused the change?

Added Activities to Give Your Project Extra Punch:

» Do the same experiment using a different kind of rock. Make sure your journal makes note of the different minerals in the rocks.

» Repeat the experiment using salt instead of rocks.

» Repeat the experiment with regular tap water. Research the water in your area and find out what minerals might be in it.

Display Extras:

» Your rocks mounted on cardboard and identified by types and properties.

» Samples of the water after it boiled from each item. Be sure to use clear containers so your visitors can compare the samples. Label them carefully.

Canned Minerals

Are minerals added to your food and drinks? They are, and it's up to you to research the subject and find out which ones. A trip to the grocery store will help you test your new knowledge and complete your project. Who knew eating rocks could be so much fun.

Do Your Research

This is a research project, not an experiment. Check with your teacher to make sure it is appropriate for your science fair. This project deals with minerals, food, and nutrition. Before you begin your project, do some research to find out more about nutrition and minerals. Once you've done some research, you can tackle this project. Or, you may come up with your own unique project.

Here are some books and websites you could start with in your research:

» Hovius, Christopher. *The Best You Can Be: A Teen's Guide to Fitness and Nutrition.* Broomall, PA: Mason Crest, 2005.

» Food and Nutrition Information Center: Vitamins & Minerals: http://www.nal.usda.gov/fnic/etext/000068.html

» Northwestern University Nutrition: Minerals: http://www.feinberg. northwestern.edu/nutrition/factsheets/minerals.html

Project Information

Possible Question:

Do packaged foods contain different minerals?

Possible Hypothesis:

Most packaged foods contain the same minerals.

Level of Difficulty:

Easy

Approximate Cost of Materials:

$5

Materials Needed:

» Notebook and pencil
» Transportation to the grocery store

Steps to Success:

1. Go to the grocery store. It is a good idea to approach the store manager and explain what you will be doing before you begin the project. If the manager objects, you should find another store. To increase your chances of getting permission, dress neatly and pick a time of day that the store is not too busy.

2. Examine several of your favorite boxed or canned food items. Try to pick a variety of foods such as cookies, pasta, chips, juice, and cereal.

3. Study the label to see if there are any minerals listed in the ingredients. You may want to bring a list of common minerals with you to the store.

4. In your notebook, write down the name of the food, including the brand, and the minerals listed in the ingredients.

Continued

Step 4

5. Make sure to write down all the foods you looked at, even if the ingredients did not list minerals.

6. At home, make a list of which minerals were most common.

7. Research these minerals and try to determine why they are in the food.

Result Summary:

» What did you learn about the minerals you researched?

» Were there more or fewer minerals than you expected to find in your favorite foods?

» Which foods had no minerals?

» What do foods without minerals have in common? What do the foods with the same minerals in them have in common?

Added Activities to Give Your Project Extra Punch:

» Read the labels of everything you eat for a week to determine what minerals you consumed in your food.

» Do some research to determine if the minerals are naturally occurring in the foods or if they were added in.

» Do some research to find out which rocks naturally contain the same minerals you might eat in your food.

» Compare different brands of foods and see if the minerals are different.

» Research minerals found in non-packaged foods such as fruits and vegetables.

Display Extras:

» Enlarged food labels with minerals listed.

» Photos of the minerals in their natural state.

» Samples of rocks that contain minerals we eat.

Are fruits and vegetables the only sources of minerals?

A Dirty Business

Some experts say elephants, hippos, and rhinos roll in wet dirt to instinctively protect their skin from the dangerous ultra violet rays of the Sun. Is mud a good sunscreen? If so, what makes it a good sunscreen? Find out with this experiment.

Do Your Research

This project requires 30 days and will work best in a sunny environment. Make sure you have enough time and sunshine to complete it. This project deals with the properties of dirt and mud and the properties of the Sun. Before you begin your project, do some research to find out about both sun damage and the properties of mud. Once you've done some research, you can tackle this project. Or, you may come up with your own unique project.

Here are some books and websites you could start with in your research:

» Barrow, Mary Mills. *Sun Protection for Life*. Oakland, CA: New Harbinger Pubs, 2005.

» How Stuff Works: Sunburn and Suntan:
http://travel.howstuffworks.com/sunscreen.htm

» Discovery Online: The Skinny on Sunscreen:
http://www.discovery.com/area/skinnyon/skinnyon970704/skinny1.html

Project Information

Possible Question:

Can wet dirt work as a sunscreen?

Possible Hypothesis:

Mud won't be as good at protecting skin as modern sunscreen.

Level of Difficulty:

Easy

Approximate Cost of Materials:

$20

Materials Needed:

» 3 pieces of leather (available at craft or fabric stores)
» 2 ounces of mud
» Rubber gloves
» Sealed container to store the mixture
» One small bottle of sunscreen
» Permanent marker
» Camera and film or digital camera

Steps to Success:

1. Draw a small circle or design on all three pieces of fabric. Make sure the three pieces of leather are all the same size, and that the circle or design is the same size on all three pieces.

2. On two of the pieces of leather place a piece of paper over the leather, except for the design.

Step 2

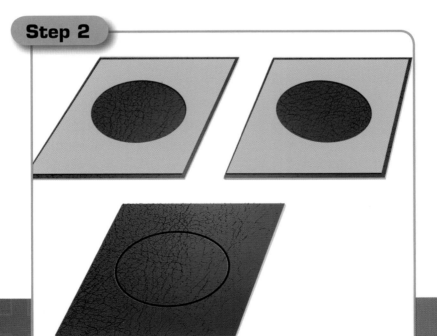

Continued

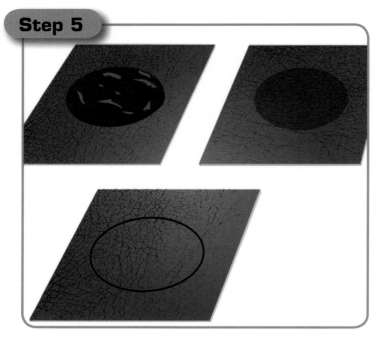

3. On one piece of leather put mud on the design. Make sure to use gloves when working with mud. On one piece of leather apply sunscreen to the design. Do not put mud or sunscreen on the piece of leather that does not have the paper cover on it.

4. Remove the paper from the leather.

5. Take a color picture of all three squares.

6. Place all three leather pieces in a sunny windowsill where they won't be disturbed for at least a month.

7. Once a week, remove the mud and sunscreen from the designs and photograph the leather.

8. Take careful notes about your observations. Is the color of the leather different inside the design than it is outside the design? Record even small details you notice.

9. Replace the mud and sunscreen and put the leather back in the windowsill. Your mud should be made from the same dirt and of the same consistency every time. You should also use sunscreen from the same bottle every time. Changing the mud or sunscreen could affect the experiment.

10. At the end of a month, remove the mud and sunscreen from the leather and take a final photograph. .

11. Compare the color of each "protected" area to see which best retained the original color and texture of the leather.

Result Summary:

» Did both designs escape the effects of the Sun? Or did one patch seem more protected than the other?

» How did the texture of the leather change under the mud and sunscreen?

» How did both substances feel against the skin of your fingertips as you applied it to the leather?

» Is mud a practical sunscreen?

Added Activities to Give Your Project Extra Punch:

» Research the composition of sunscreen. Does it contain any of the same minerals as your mud?

» Research sunscreens sold as "natural" or "organic." What minerals do they consist of? What makes them natural?

» Research other naturally occurring substances that are used as sunscreen.

Display Extras:

» Find pictures of animals in their natural habitats covered with mud.

» Display your commercial sunscreen, your mud, and your leather scraps, as well as the photos you've included in your journal notes.

» Use images of the sun.

Hopefully these people are all wearing sunscreen!

The Competition

Learning is it's own reward, but winning the science fair is pretty fun, too. Here are some things to keep in mind if you want to do well in competition:

1) Creativity counts. Do not simply copy an experiment from this or any other book. You need to change the experiment so that it is uniquely your own.

2) You will need to be able to explain your project to the judges. Being able to talk intelligently about your work will help reassure the judges that you learned something and did the work yourself. You may have to repeat the same information to different judges, so make sure you've practiced it ahead of time. You will also need to be able to answer the judge's questions about your methods and results.

3) You will need to present your materials in an appealing manner. Discuss with your teacher whether or not it is acceptable to have someone help you with artistic flourishes to your display.

Keep these guidelines in mind for your display:

» **Type and print:** Display the project title, the question, the hypothesis, and the collected data in clean, neatly crafted paper printouts that you can mount on a sturdy poster display.

» **Visibility:** Be sure you print your title and headings in large type and in energetic colors. If your project is about the sun, maybe you'll use bright reds, oranges, and yellows to bring your letters to life. If your project is about plant life, maybe you'll use greens and browns to capture an earthy mood. You want your project to be easily visible in a crowd of other projects.

» **Standing display:** Be sure your display can stand on its own. Office supply stores have thick single-, double-, and triple-section display boards available in several sizes and colors that will work nicely as the canvas for your science fair masterpiece. Mount your core data — your discoveries — on this display, along with photos and other relevant materials (charts, resource articles, interviews, etc.).

» **Dress neatly and comfortably for the fair.** You may be standing on your feet for a long time.

4) The final report is an important part of your project. Make sure the following things are in your final report:

» **A title page:** the first page of your report, with your name and the name of your project (similar to page 1 of this book)

» **A table of contents:** what's included in your report (similar to page 3 of this book)

» **Research:** the research you did that led you to choose this topic and help you to formulate your question

» **Your project question:** what you tested

» **Your hypothesis:** your prediction of how your experiment would answer the question

» **Materials:** the things you used to conduct your experiment

» **Methods:** the steps you took to perform your experiment

» **Observations:** some of the things you recorded in your research journal

» **Conclusion:** how closely your hypothesis lined up with the results

» **Bibliography:** books, articles, and other resources you used in researching and preparing your project. Discuss with your teacher the appropriate way to list your sources.

» **Acknowledgments:** recognition of those who helped you to prepare and work on your project

Prepare to Be Judged

Each science fair is different but you will probably be assigned points based on the categories below. Make sure to talk to your teacher about how your specific science fair will be judged. Ask yourself the questions in each category to see if you've done the best possible job.

Your objectives
» Did you present original, creative ideas?
» Did you state the problem or question clearly?
» Did you define the variables and use controls?
» Did you relate your research to the problem or question?

Your skills
» Do you understand your results?
» Did you do your own work? It's OK for an adult to help you for safety reasons, but not to do the work for you. If you cannot explain the experiment, the equipment, and the steps you took, the judges may not believe you did your own work.

Data collection and interpretation
» Did you keep a research journal?
» Was your experiment planned correctly to collect what you needed?
» Did you correctly interpret your results?
» Could someone else repeat the experiment?
» Are your conclusions based only on the results of your experiment?

Presentation
» Is your display attractive and complete?
» Do you have a complete report?
» Did you use reliable sources and document them correctly?
» Can you answer questions about your work?

Glossary

absorbent able to take in water

aquifer underground layer that holds and releases water

control something that is left unchanged in order to compare results against it

data factual information

geologic related to Earth

hypothesis informed guess based on evidence

pollutant residue that causes something to be unclean

pore small opening that matter can pass through

prediction to say in advance what you think will happen, based on scientific study

scientific theory belief based on tested evidence and facts

sedimentary rock formed from layers of dirt that have been washed downstream over a very long period of time

variable element in an experiment that can change

Index

absorbency 20–23
acid rain 12–15
acknowledgments 45
aquifers 24–27

bibliographies 45
books 8, 12, 16, 20, 24, 28, 32, 36, 40

clothing 44
competition 44
conclusions 45, 46
control groups 6
controlled variables 6
creativity 44

dependent variables 6
displays 11, 15, 19, 23, 27, 31, 35, 39, 43, 44, 46

erosion 12–15

field guides 11, 34
final report 45
foods 36–39

halite 28
hypotheses
  absorbency 21
  acid rain 13
  aquifers 25
  display of 44
  erosion 13
  final report and 45
  formation of 5, 7
  mineral water 33

minerals in foods 37
mud as
  sunscreen 41
rock classification 9
salt and plants 29
sedimentary
  rocks 21
smooth rocks 17

independent
  variables 6
Internet 4, 5

judging 44, 46

materials
  absorbency 21
  acid rain 13
  aquifers 25
  erosion 13
  final report and 45
  mineral water 33
  minerals in foods 37
mud as
  sunscreen 41
rock classification 9
salt and plants 29
sedimentary
  rocks 21
smooth rocks 17
mineral water 32–35
minerals 28–31, 32–35, 36–39
Mohs hardness scale 8, 9, 10
mud, as sunscreen 40–43

nitrogen oxides
  (NO_x) 14
notes 7

observations 45

pollutants 12
pores 20
project information
  absorbency 21
  acid rain 13
  aquifers 25
  erosion 13
  mineral water 33
  minerals in foods 37
mud as
  sunscreen 41
rock classification 9
salt and plants 29
sedimentary
  rocks 21
smooth rocks 17
project journals 46

research 4, 8, 12, 16, 20, 24, 28, 32, 36, 40, 45
research journals 7
result summaries
  absorbency 23
  acid rain 15
  aquifers 27
  erosion 15
  mineral water 35
  minerals in foods 39
mud as
  sunscreen 43

rock classification 11
salt and plants 31
sedimentary
  rocks 23
smooth rocks 19
rock classification
  8–11
rules 6

salt, plants and 28–31
scientific predictions 7
scientific questions
  4, 5
scientific theory 4
search engines 4
sedimentary rocks
  20–23
smooth rocks 16–19
sulfur dioxide (SO_2) 14

table of contents 45
title pages 45

variables 6, 7

websites 8, 12, 16, 20, 24, 28, 32, 36, 40